ADVENT THIRST ... CHRISTMAS HOPE

Prayer and Meditation for the Journey

by Anita M. Constance, S.C.

D0064446

 PAULIST PRESS · New York/Mahwah

Cover design and interior illustrations by Anne Haarer, S.C.

Excerpts are taken from the *Lectionary for Mass* copyright © 1970 Confraternity of Christian Doctrine, Washington, D.C. All rights reserved.

Library of Congress Cataloging-in-Publication Data

Constance, Anita, 1945–
    Advent thirst—Christmas hope : prayer and meditation for the journey / by Anita Constance.
    p. cm.
    ISBN 0-8091-3511-6 (pbk.)
    1. Advent—Prayer-books and devotions—English. 2. Advent—Meditations. 3. Christmas—Prayer-books and devotions—English. 4. Christmas—Meditations. I. Title.
    BV40.C55 1994
    242'.33—dc20   94-16328
                                               CIP

Published by Paulist Press
997 Macarthur Boulevard
Mahwah, N.J. 07430

Printed and bound in the United States of America

DEDICATION

To the Sisters of Charity of Saint Elizabeth
Women of Faith, Love and Vision

INTRODUCTION

Winter makes everything seem like a wilderness. Gardens are replaced by patches of cold, hard earth. One would never know that they had the potential to be anything. Our lives are sometimes like that. There are times we look inside ourselves, through the eyes of winter's bleakness, and see a wilderness. But, in truth, the wilderness is not a wasteland. It is merely that place deep within us as yet untouched, uncultivated by our efforts to turn over the soil that would reveal the richness that lies beneath.

During Advent a voice cries out that urges us to see past the cold earth, to deep within, and realize that we have potential . . . potential to grow and bear fruit. But, first, the soil of our lives needs to be turned over, converted, so that the seeds of our dreams and desires can come into reality. The potential is there, but there are still corners of that wilderness within that require more work. And so, we come to this season of Advent with a sense of humility and dependence on God.

Mother Teresa of Calcutta once said, "God does not call us to be successful. He calls us to be faithful." Fidelity requires patience, and the most difficult person to be patient with is ourselves . . . especially when we want to make changes. We want success, and we want it now. It is hard to accept the fact that growth is a lifelong process, and that we will be called to look into our lives again and again. But if we are faithful in trying to do just that, we will begin a chain reaction . . . a change reaction in the world around us. Even while our efforts might be for ourselves and our relationship with God, we affect others.

The truth is, Advent isn't just four weeks, it is every day. Every day we are called to prepare the ground of our being so that it will become the "good earth." We wait and we long, and yet we work as we long. We pay attention to our lived experience and, with God's grace, uncover the reign of God—fashion it in the ways of God. So we carry our Advent thirst through the hope of Christmas and beyond. We are invited to touch lifelong desires, celebrate hopes fulfilled and live with promise in our hearts.

We wait and we long
for you, O God.
Yet, we question
whether we are worthy
of your coming.

We wait and we long
for you, O God.
But we grow restless
in the waiting—
impatient with your
sense of timing.

We wait and we long
for you, O God.
Yet we fear
the majesty of your return—
for truly
the heavens would break open,
and the mountains quake
in your presence.
And we,
we would see ourselves
as we truly are.

Yet, we wait and we long
for you, O God.
For we dare not miss
the day, the hour,
the moment.

AND WE LONG

And while we wait,
we trust—
for you are
a loving creator
who touched the earth,
and consecrated the ground
of our being.

You hold and mold
us gently,
so gently, at times,
that we are unaware.
Yet the work continues
as we wait and long.

Loving God,
may your faith in us
lead us to faith in you.
Help us to accept the darkness,
to believe
what eye has not seen
and ear has not heard,
and to sense our hearts
in the hollow
of your hands—
that we might not
grow weary or discouraged
as we wait and long
for you. Amen.

The days are coming, says the Lord, when I will fulfill the promise I made.... (Jer 33:14)

A promise, kept or broken, is a very important piece in the mosaic of human relationships. It evokes expectation in the heart of the one who receives it, because a promise is grounded in trust.

Trust, hope, expectancy are the foundation and bedrock of the lives of a pilgrim people. In setting out on our journey to the kingdom, we commit ourselves to a lifetime advent. For on the way, we will meet our own hungers and thirst ... our own deserts. We will come face to face with desire and disappointment. But with promise in our "traveling bag," we have the courage to strain forward toward fulfillment, the journey's end.

Jeremiah is a man of promise. He is an instrument of hope and fulfillment. Reluctant to speak in the name of the Lord, it was his trust in the promise of God that enabled him to loosen his grasp on self-concern and become the utterance of God. We, too, can trust in the promise—the faithful love of God. We, too, can become prophets and instruments of love, hope and justice in the world. The days are here. The time is now. The promise is fulfilled.

Prayer

Lord of promise,
God of fulfillment,
enable us to trust
what we do not see.
Give us courage
along the way,
as we make our
advent journey.

Let us not grow weary,
but walk this lifetime
with our eyes fixed
on the horizon just ahead—
that place where
heaven and earth meet,
that place where
truth and justice kiss. Amen.

Reflection

How has God's promise of fidelity affected my life?

....

....

....

....

....

What have been God's personal promises to me?

....

....

....

....

....

What are the areas of my life in which God has given me hope?

....

....

....

....

....

Jesus said to him, "I will come and cure him." "Sir," the centurion said in reply, "I am not worthy...." (Mt 8:7-8)

Jesus is there for the asking. But sometimes his gracious spontaneity takes us by surprise. The centurion replied, "I am not worthy," but did that matter to the Lord? Did that block his generous spirit? All Jesus seeks is an open heart. We could say he looks for a heart in need. He waits to be invited into broken places, soul-filled yearnings. Jesus came to heal us and to set us free. He is not interested in our measuring-up, self-imposed standards. He enters the home of our being willingly. Worthiness is not an issue for him. Love is.

When we pray, "Come, Lord Jesus," during this season of Advent, do we truly believe that he will come? Come into our lives, our homes, our neighborhoods, our world? Come at the end of time? Do we believe in what we pray? We can believe it because God loves invitations.

Prayer

Healing God,
touch us
at our point of anguish
this day—
that place
which is known
only to you,
that place
which can be touched
only by you.

No one else
could find that place
and know it to be so—
even we
are unsure
of the broken places
and wounded spaces
within.

Healing God,
touch us
at our point of anguish
this day. Amen.

Reflection

What are the broken places and soul-filled yearnings in my life?

....

....

....

....

....

....

Have I invited the healing Christ into those wounded spaces? If not,
why?

....

....

....

....

....

....

Not by appearance shall he judge, nor by hearsay shall he decide. (Is 11:3)

    Our deepest longing is satisfied in the words of the prophet Isaiah. To be accepted as we are—to know that someone, God, will look into our hearts and say, "Yes." Another advent desire is fulfilled. We are released from our fears of inadequacy. We are set free by hope itself. Our failures will no longer be the measure of our value and worth. Our attempts at goodness and love will be valued beyond their, sometimes feeble, accomplishments. A "third person" tale will not be enough for God.

    Now we can say freely, safely, "Here I am, Lord." Here *I* am. No longer afraid that who I am is of no interest to God. Who I am is the very person in whom God is most interested. For, at this point of origin, our truest self, we are "created love." As we move toward God, we journey from that point of origin ... that image and likeness of God. What better place to start!

Prayer

Creator God,
take us to the place
that you call home.
Let us no longer
be strangers
in a foreign land—
aliens to our very selves.

Forgive us
for the times
that we lost
faith in our beginnings.

You see us
as we are.
You know us better
than we know ourselves.
In your mercy,
gift us with the joy
of our creation
that we may know
as we are known.

Lead us
from our years
of desert and discontent
to the place of promise
we hold within. Amen.

Reflection

How do I feel when I do not have to defend or prove myself to another? To God?

....

....

....

....

....

How can I better respect and appreciate my value, the value I share with others?

....

....

....

....

....

How will we ever get enough bread in this deserted spot to satisfy such a crowd? (Mt 15:33)

The disciples were overwhelmed by the number of people in need that day, but Jesus did not want to send them away hungry. We, too, are overwhelmed by the hunger and poverty of the world around us. Where do we begin? How can we possibly satisfy so many? As we sit in our fine homes and eat our more than adequate meals, we look at the crowd and grow more and more uncomfortable. What can we do?

Jesus provides the solution to this gnawing dilemma. "How many loaves of bread do you have?" he asked them. In other words, begin with what you have. If you want to satisfy even a few, what is it that you can share? What is the "more than enough" in your life that creates the imbalance for our brothers and sisters? Begin there. It will be different for each one of us. But that is the place to start. How will we ever get enough? We probably won't if we keep our eyes on the crowd and never look to ourselves.

Prayer

God of fullness
and plenty,
draw us into the
world beyond ourselves.
Help us
to take from
the storehouse
of what we have
and who we are,
and extend the feast
of our tables—
to reach
our brothers and sisters
in hunger and need.

It is so easy
to be tricked
by inadequacy.
Let us not
use impossibility
as an excuse
not to begin. Amen.

Reflection

What needs of others overwhelm my life?

....
....
....
....

How do I seek to help the poor and the oppressed?

....
....
....
....

How do I name them?

....
....
....

THURSDAY *First* WEEK OF ADVENT

Blessed is he who comes in the name of the Lord. (Ps 118:26)

We are ambassadors of Christ, Paul said. We come in the name of the Lord. That is quite a responsibility. But before we think of the responsibility, do we realize that we are blessed—that we live under the blessing of God? We should not be overwhelmed, then, but confident. We do not move forward with our own agenda, but with the reign of God as our bill of fare. We do not fulfill that purpose and task alone, but under the strength and guidance of the Spirit. We do not speak merely human words, but truly the word of God. So, blessed are WE who come in the name of the Lord!

Because of this, we can move through our lives as if on the threshold of something new-about-to-happen. We can live this Advent experience with expectation and assurance . . . seeing through the eyes of grace, knowing that what we touch and what touches us is truly the caress of blessedness.

Prayer

Blessed God,
we, who are
the reflection of you,
bow before
the sacredness
of this earth
and one another—
blessing and blessed.

We ask you
for new awareness
of your presence
within and
around us.

We come
in your name—
the name of our Creator,
Redeemer and Life-Giver.
Help us to recognize
your blessings
and our blessedness.
Let us be free
and light of heart
as we walk this earth . . .
as we proclaim
the good news
of your reign today. Amen.

Reflection

How am I a blessing of God in the lives of others?

....

....

....

How are they the blessing of God to me?

....

....

....

....

In what ways am I effecting the reign of God?

....

....

....

....

Jesus said to them, "Are you confident that I can do this?"
(Mt 9:28)

"Do you believe me?" asks Jesus. "Do you really believe?" It seems to be a simple enough question, but it is packed with power. Everything in us comes to bear on that moment of decision. It is that crucial hour between doubt and faith, hesitancy and confidence, mistrust and abandon. What is most important is on the line. The gospel response is also very simple—"Yes." Just one word, but was that "yes" spoken without a struggle? I do not think so. Commitment does not come easily.

What, then, led the blind men in today's gospel to faith and confidence? Grace ... grace touched the eyes of their hearts long before Jesus restored their vision. Grace met them on the road and led them to Jesus ... led them to ask for healing. Grace showed them that real seeing meant believing. Asking, itself, was the first step because faith lives in the quiet corners of desire.

Perhaps the eyes of our hearts need to be touched by grace, too. Then, in some particular way this Advent, we might better see the birth of Christ in everyday living. Deep faith and holy expectation are Advent gifts we will receive ... if we do the asking.

Prayer

Faithful God,
meet us
on the road
with graces
for the journey.

Let us be willing
to ask the question—
to place
our heart's desire
into your hands.

Give us
the courage to ask,
the humility
to feel the longing,
and the joy
of waiting in faith.
May we surrender
our doubt
to holy expectation
and abandon our disbelief
to hope-filled trust. Amen.

Reflection

Do I invite grace to touch my vision that I might see a better world and a better "me"?

....

Where am I in need of believing . . . with hope and confidence?

....

....

....

....

....

How might I fill that need? How might Jesus?

....

....

....

....

....

....

No longer will your Teacher hide himself. (Is 30:20)

"When the student is ready, the Teacher appears." This saying should keep us from worry and anxiety because it seems, in all good timing (God's timing), God raises up someone who will show us the way. The Israelites were longing for the Messiah, a Savior, but when Jesus came along they did not recognize him. They missed their Teacher and Lord.

When we pray for God to show us the way, do we sometimes miss the person or situation God provides for us? Are we so set in the ways we want to be helped, a criterion or plan, that the answer to our prayers walks by unnoticed?

We sometimes catch ourselves wishing we lived in the time of Christ, thinking we would recognize him and accept him, but would we really? Perhaps those teacher-reflections of him have walked among us, moved in and out of our lives. If they did, there are probably more to come. Now is the time to start paying attention.

Prayer

Hidden God,
you reveal yourself
mysteriously.
Free us from
the need to touch
your presence clearly.
Free us, that our eyes
might see you
in unexpected places
and undetermined ways.

Let us not miss
the visible signs
of your presence,
lest we cling to
illusions or dreams.
Rather, make us ready
to meet the companions
and teachers
who greet us
on our journey. Amen.

Reflection

Most recently, who has entered my life as a sign of God's presence?

....

....

....

....

....

....

....

How might I ensure that I will not miss my Teacher and God in the everyday?

....

....

....

....

....

....

....

Make ready the way of the Lord. (Lk 3:4)

Advent is a time of anticipation, a time for looking forward. But John the Baptist reminds us that we must first look within, reflect upon our lives and the changes that will prepare us for the return of Jesus. Change is a call and a challenge to grow, but it is also a reality of life itself. To live is to change and to grow is to change much.

John went into the desert, willing to view his life in perspective. He was dedicated to honesty, admitting the shadows he found cast in his heart by the presence of Jesus. He acknowledged who he was and recognized his need to change and grow.

We, too, are called to be people of change, people dedicated to growth. Leaving the desert, John shouted the words of the prophet Isaiah. We hear those words today.... What are the mountains in our lives that need to be leveled? Are they pride or prejudice, perhaps? What valleys need to be filled in? Are they lows of despair or emptiness? What wilderness needs to be cleared to prepare for the return of the Lord?

Advent is a time in the desert, but not a time to escape into solitude. It is a time to walk into our hearts and to notice the shifting sands of our lives. And, finally, to leave that place a bit changed and ready to make a difference.

Prayer

God of newness,
Lord of change,
keep us faithful
to the process
of life
that bids us
to grow—
to be holy
and whole.

Continue to bring us
to that quiet place within,
and, there, show us
who we are—
not to condemn us
but to offer
the hospitality
of fullness and life.

Grant that
we may yield
to the sands of time
that sift through our hearts—
softening edges
and rubbing us
smooth . . .
that we might be
a better fit
in the palm
of your hand. Amen.

Reflection

What is my attitude toward the weaknesses and inconsistencies of my life?

. . . .

. . . .

. . . .

. . . .

. . . .

Do I believe in my potential for change and growth?

. . . .

. . . .

. . . .

We have seen incredible things today. (Lk 5:26)

The people who witnessed the healing of the paralytic were amazed. They knew they were present to the extraordinary, and they willingly acknowledged it. Perhaps the healing and forgiveness of sins, though, overshadowed a less obvious blessing in the life of the paralytic—the blessing of real friendship. The crowd was present to this, too. Think of the care and love of this man's friends for a moment. Such extraordinary concern and determination that they would do anything to bring their friend to Jesus! It wasn't only the faith of the paralytic that impressed Jesus, it was their's as well . . . faith in miracles, but also faith in the power of love. Could Jesus resist this affirmation of human life? Never!

We are not alone on our journey to God. We are not alone in building God's kingdom or living God's reign in our hearts. We have each other. Today's display of human affection touches us. Perhaps we need to look to our left and right, as we walk along, to become more aware of our companions on this journey. This example of friendship should remind us of those we have in our own lives. Let us thank God for the love and faith we share with them. Let us thank God for the times they brought us to Jesus in prayer. Let us thank God for the incredible things—the blessings—of real friendship.

Prayer

Loving God,
giver of
all good gifts,
keep us mindful
of the blessings
of one another.
Keep us
from the fear
of loneliness,
for always
there is someone
by our side.
We need only
to turn and to see.

Your covenant
of friendship
has enabled us
to cherish
faithful love.
May that love
shower
blessings upon us
as we remain
faithful to one another
and to the
gifts that we share. Amen.

Reflection

Who are the friends that have brought me closer to God?

....
....
....
....

How might I pray for each one?
What might I ask for each individual?

....
....
....
....
....
....

Will he not leave the ninety-nine out on the hills and go in search of the stray? (Mt 18:12)

What a comforting thought! The Good Shepherd would leave all that he has to search for the one that he hasn't. What is missing must be found! When we stray from the Lord's side, that is reason enough for Jesus to seek us out. We might not even be aware that we are lost. He is aware and that is enough. How generous of God to go out and find us before we even know the need to be found!

Perhaps the lost sheep really thought the grass was greener someplace else. Sometimes we do, too, and off we go looking for that "something more." Why can't we be satisfied with what we have? Why can't we be satisfied with remaining by the side of our Savior and Lord?

We all have our reasons, but none of them is reason enough for God to allow us to stray too far or stay away too long. Jesus will always bring us back to the rolling hills of his peace and reintroduce us to the safety of his presence.

Prayer

God of the lost,
seeker of the human heart,
never cease
to know us better
than we know ourselves.

When your presence
is not enough
for us,
show us compassion.
Set out
on the search
and find us.
No matter what, find us—
for we want
to be found.

We rely
on your tender
understanding
and your merciful
forgiveness.
May we hear
your call
and turn
to meet you
as you draw near.
Lift us up
and bring us home.
Place us gently
by your side,
that we may
rest in your peace. Amen.

Reflection

When was the last time I experienced God's loving concern for me?

. . . .

. . . .

. . . .

. . . .

. . . .

What might stand in the way of this experience of God for me?

. . . .

. . . .

. . . .

. . . .

. . . .

Jesus said, "Come to me, all you who are weary and find life burdensome, and I will refresh you." (Mt 11:28)

How many times have we heard those words and found strength in just the hearing? When life is a little heavy and our hearts yearn for a more gentle touch, the hand of Jesus reaches out to lift the burden. His remedy is simple, "Come to me." If we but place that burden of ours down for a moment and sit at the feet of Jesus, he will teach us how to ease our souls and rest our spirits.

The journey can be long, the road rough, the days dreary at times. But it is then that Jesus says, "Come to me." No, Jesus will not force himself upon us, but he is the God of hospitality. He invites us into the home of his heart. He wants us to sit down at his table of refreshment and peace. "Come to me," he tells us. Let us take him at his word, for he will never disappoint our longing.

Prayer

God of peace,
let us rest
easy
within you.
We come
weary from
the day's heat
and the night's cold.

We seek
refreshment
for our spirits
and gentleness
for our souls.

May we hear
your invitation
to enter
your presence
and
lay our burdens down.
Give us the grace
of healing life
that we may
rise, once again,
and walk on
with the lightness
of your love. Amen.

Reflection

Has life become a distraction or burden for me, rather than a gift?

....

....

....

....

....

How might I respond to the hospitality of Jesus so that I will learn
more about the gift that life is?

....

....

....

....

....

....

I am the Lord, your God, who grasp your right hand. (Is 41:13)

To be grasped by God is to be grasped by Truth... and the truth will set us free. To be grasped by God is to be grasped by Love... and love never ends. To be grasped by God is to be grasped by Compassion... and compassion leads to acceptance.

To be grasped by Truth, Love and Compassion is only one side of the equation of our lives. The other side resides within ourselves. To be grasped by Truth asks commitment to the truth—the truth of God and the truth of ourselves... that God is Creator and we are creation... that we are totally dependent, but God is totally dependable. God's grasp is truly an embrace that holds us.

To be grasped by Love asks commitment to love—to a generous God but also to ourselves as receivers of the gift. Are we committed to the freedom of being loved? Are we committed to love one another freely? To be empowered and to empower?

To be grasped by Compassion asks commitment to compassion —to know that we are accepted and to reach out to others, knowing that we have been forgiven much. To reach out to others with God's "Yes"—to affirm all life, all existence, in the face of interpersonal darkness and misunderstanding.

To be grasped by God is to be held fast, steadfastly, in the ways of God!

Prayer

God of Truth,
give us peace
in the knowledge
that you are God.
Let us rejoice
in our creation
that we might
lean into
the hollow
of your hands.

God of Love,
give us freedom
in the knowledge
that we rest
within your heart.

Let us be
caught up
in your
flame of love
that we might
spark life
into souls
who yearn for
your creative embrace.

God of Compassion,
give us healing
in the knowledge
of acceptance by you.
Let us affirm
one another,
ever mindful that
we have been looked upon
with eyes of mercy. Amen.

Reflection

How have I expressed commitment to truth, love and compassion this
past year?

....

....

....

How have I experienced my dependence and God's dependability?
My love empowering another and another's love empowering me?
My compassion affirming another and another's affirming me?

....

....

....

He is like a tree planted near running water, that yields its fruit in due season. (Ps 1:3)

Nature offers us much wisdom in the cycle of the seasons. Each one offers its own "fruitfulness," its own lesson, about life itself. But in general, they teach us that time cannot be rushed. Time takes time. Winter would do violence to summer, if it were not for spring. Summer fades slowly into winter by the grace of autumn. And spring gives birth to summer in the slow awakening of new life.

We, too, yield our fruitfulness in due season. We are a part of nature, a human nature, and we waltz to the same rhythm of seasons and fulfillment. The passage of time demands our respect and acceptance, for life, death and new life are natural, human, Christian mysteries. We must not do violence to that inner waltz of time. In many ways, we have no choice—we cannot rush the due seasons of our lives.

So we must dance in the darkness, at times, until our season comes... trusting the wisdom of God who has written the music of our creation.

Prayer

God of wisdom,
Lord of time,
you teach us
about the mysteries
of life
through the steady
fulfillment
of your creation.

Time passes
in the gentle
sweep of seasons.
Minutes and hours
melt into
days, weeks, years
of dynamic sameness.

Nature
embraces us
in its rhythm
of birth, death and new life.

Give us the grace
of the seasons, Lord.
Let us be
gentle and patient
with the passage
of time
that we might
ripen into resurrection—
having first accepted
the depths of darkness—
to welcome
the dawn of new life. Amen.

Reflection

What seems to be pressing or pressuring to me at this time?

....
....
....
....
....

How can I let go and be open to the timeless within my heart?

....
....
....
....
....

Take care of this vine, and protect what your right hand has planted. (Ps 80:16)

In a loving act of creation God "planted" us on this earth. Today we ask God to protect what has been planted. Sometimes we are very in touch with our weakness and powerlessness. We seek courage and strength. Sometimes our lives feel rootless and dried up. We long for flowing waters of grace to quench our thirsting spirits. We cry out, "Take care of this vine, O Lord, and protect what your right hand has planted."

At times like these we may wonder where the Divine Gardener is. But then there comes a slow, quiet realization that we have not been forgotten. Just when we feel we have sunk to the depths, the hand of God reaches down to support the vine of our lives. It is a gentle lifting of our spirits, but there is, clearly, a recognizable, felt experience of God's presence. The truth is, we have been resting in God all along. For, even more than being the Divine Gardener, God is also the very ground of our being.

Prayer

God of our longing,
being calls
to Being.
Lift us
from the parched earth
of our weakness
and frailty.
Pour out
the flowing waters
of your Spirit,
that our souls
may drink their fill.

Soften
the ground of our being
with your
healing touch
and
let your Son
shine within us,
so that what
you have planted
may bear
much fruit. Amen.

Reflection

Am I willing to cry out my need, or do I keep God and others from knowing my emptiness?

. . . .

. . . .

In what ways, at what times, have I known God's faithfulness?

. . . .

. . . .

. . . .

. . . .

. . . .

. . . .

. . . .

. . . .

. . . .

. . . .

The Lord is near. Dismiss all anxiety from your minds.
(Phil 4:6)

The gift of presence is both comforting and reassuring. To have someone near in times of anxiety and uncertainty lessens the fears of anticipation as we face the unknown. Sometimes, words are not possible. Often, they are not necessary, for when people are truly present to each other they can hear the silent messages of the heart. And it is the heart that beats to the rhythm of life's sadness and joy. What a gift to have someone unconditionally present in life!

During Advent, as we anticipate the return of God's presence enfleshed, let us not forget that divine presence with us every day. That is God's loving gift to us in Jesus Christ. The Lord is near, today—now—present in the rhythm of our sadness and joy, present in the stillness of what is yet unknown.

Prayer

Ever-present God,
you are the gift
of eternal nearness,
yet we often question
where you are.
Our hearts grow anxious
as we search for you.
We grope in darkness
and long with
deep desire for your touch.
But you are near.
You hear us in the quiet.
You stretch forth your hand
to reach us
when we wander
from your side.

Let us find comfort
in your faithful love.
Open our ears
that we may hear you.
Warm our hearts
that we may feel you.
Calm our fears
that we, too, may
reach out and meet
your healing touch. Amen.

Reflection

When do I experience acceptance? With whom?

....

....

....

....

....

Do I feel I must measure up to some standard before I am accepted
by others, by God? If so, what might God say to me about this?

....

....

....

....

....

I see him, though not now; I behold him, though not near.
(Nm 24:17)

Are these contradictory statements or is there a truth which underlies a mystery? To see and behold God is impossible in this life. Yet we are told the impossible is possible. If Emmanuel is God-with-us, how could we not know that presence? Perhaps we limit our true experience. Perhaps we are short-sighted or unaware of the deeper vision we all possess which can see beyond the obvious and the concrete.

The truth is God *is* with us. The mystery is not so much a puzzle to be solved, but a love too deep to be fathomed. Perhaps the answer lies in surrender—the acceptance of that love.

Prayer

God of nearness,
the mystery of your presence
burns in our hearts
like fire
that hungers to consume
the barrenness of
winter's cold—
for we long to see
your face.

Help us to surrender
to your love
present in our every day—
gentle as a summer's breeze,
yet powerful enough
to penetrate the night
that blinds us
to the nearness of you.
Open our eyes to mystery
and our hearts to the
gift of your loving embrace.
Amen.

Reflection

Have I viewed my longing for God as God's absence, or as an experience of God's presence?

....

....

....

....

....

What limits my vision of this?

....

....

....

....

....

....

....

When the afflicted man called out, the Lord heard, and from all his distress God saved him. (Ps 34:7)

Sometimes we question whether the Lord hears our cries for help. The words of today's psalm express no doubt about it, though. For the psalmist, it was a proven fact based on experience. And there is only one requirement for the presence of God in times of need— that we turn to God, acknowledging that emptiness or helplessness.

It seems that God looks to be invited. It is not that God will only meet us halfway, but voicing our need emphasizes the depth of our commitment, our total reliance on the Lord of love. God does not need us to be vulnerable, but when we are we have an even greater capacity for God's abiding care.

Prayer

Abiding God,
life and heart
of heaven and earth,
touch our lips
with the burning coals
of our desire for you.

Let the circumstances
of our lives
not keep us from you.
May they be
not the emptiness
of a well—
but the wellspring
of your love
and saving power.

Sustain us
when we believe
that we can never
be sustained.
Free us
when the burdens of life
seem to shackle us
with unfreedom.
Bid us come to you
in our times of
deafness and need—
that the salvation of God,
our brother Jesus Christ,
may visit us. Amen.

Reflection

Am I willing to acknowledge my needs before God? Before others?
What are those needs this day?

. . . .

. . . .

. . . .

. . . .

. . . .

. . . .

Can I believe that they might reveal God to me . . . be an opportunity
for grace?

. . . .

. . . .

. . . .

Kindness and truth shall meet; justice and peace shall kiss.
(Ps 85:11)

We look forward to many things during the season of Advent. Psalm 85 arouses a deep longing that speaks to fulfillment of the human heart. Are any of these ideals really possible? Are these truly hopes or merely wishes? The answer to those questions resides within us.

We are the meeting place of kindness and truth, justice and peace. We are where dreams become reality, and ideals have possibility. It is we who make things like truth and justice come to be... through human living. If I want truth to be, I must "be" in truth. If I want justice to be, I must be just. If I want peace to reign, it must first reign in my heart. If I want love to be, I must live in love.

The formula is simple enough. The living requires commitment and perseverance. With God, all things are possible.

Prayer

Lord of hope,
God of possibilities,
we dedicate ourselves
to the reign
of your kingdom on earth.

We stand before you
as a people
entrusted with the
character of this kingdom.
We lift our eyes
to the heavens

and await the grace
of courage. . . .
We pray for it
to tumble down
into our hearts.

Be with us
as we walk the road
to justice and peace.
Fill our hearts
with the flame of kindness
and the light of truth. Amen.

Reflection

Can I see my infinite longings as longings for God?
Do I believe that they hold the possibility of fulfillment?

. . . .

. . . .

. . . .

. . . .

. . . .

What can I do to bring about their fulfillment?
How might I invite God into these longings?

. . . .

. . . .

. . . .

. . . .

. . . .

. . . .

. . . .

THURSDAY *Third* WEEK OF ADVENT

My love shall never leave you, nor my covenant of peace be shaken. (Is 54:10)

One can almost taste the power behind this promise of God . . . to never leave us. God's covenant of peace will never be destroyed! No matter what may occur on this earth, whether natural disaster or failing of the human heart, God will never forsake us. God will never fail in faithfulness. The strength of God's word, through the prophet Isaiah, is but a taste of God's determined love and acceptance to be found in the Word of Jesus the Son.

As we approach the celebration of the Word-made-flesh, we are encouraged to reflect upon the times we have experienced this faithfulness of God. We are called to look at God's fidelity in the face of our infidelity. God's generous presence, when we are unaware of that presence. Perhaps we will find ourselves giving thanks. Perhaps we will find ourselves silent in the face of such unconditional love.

Prayer

Never-failing God,
keeper of promises
and faithful in love,
draw us into
your steadfast heart.

Prepare us for the
coming of your Son,
Jesus Christ.
Quiet our minds.
Bid us be still
and cease
the endless activity
of our days—

for just a little while ...
that we might think
of you.

Let us feel
the breath of your Spirit
as it fills the earth.
Let us breathe in deeply
and sigh
at its gentle touch
of peace.
We ask this,
mindful of your presence,
in heartfelt desire for you.
Amen.

Reflection

What place of hiding or fear, within me, does God wish to speak to
with unconditional love?

. . . .

. . . .

. . . .

. . . .

. . . .

How can I place it before God? What could I ask for or say? What does
God say to me?

. . . .

. . . .

. . . .

. . . .

. . . .

For my house shall be called a house of prayer for all peoples.
(Is 56:7)

    "Let us pray ..." and obediently we bow our heads. Do we do this so often and so easily that we do not take prayer as seriously as we should? Jesus did not take prayer lightly. He valued this communication with God. It was the opportunity for him to abide in the presence of the Father—and, there, to find strength, peace and hope.

    We may be convinced of the necessity of prayer in our lives, but sometimes we feel it "doesn't seem to be working" for us. Maybe we're tempted to throw the blame on God. Why not? We seem to be doing our part. Perhaps that is the problem. We may be looking at prayer as a contract with God, rather than the experience of a relationship.

    Jesus called us friends. In friendship, we speak to another from the heart. When sharing, we share ourselves ... what we feel inside. We are open, honest, even vulnerable, at times. Isn't this the way we should be with God, with Jesus? What we celebrate, each Christmas, is God coming to us in the helplessness and dependency of a newborn child. Perhaps that is how God would like us to reach out in prayer. For then, each touch would be nothing less than God's caress of our child within.

Prayer

Gentle Lord,
help us to be
as little children
cradled in the assurance
of your mother
and father touch.

Let us not fear
to cry in need
or to laugh with joy
in your presence.
Teach us how to pray.

May we know you
in friendship love—
love that says "yes"
to our weakness
and our strengths,
to our richness
and our poverty.
Give us confidence
in your care
and courage
in our vulnerability.
Let us turn to you,
who have already
turned to us. Amen.

Reflection

Am I open to God with my needs, or do I fear disappointment?

....

....

....

Am I uncomfortable with the silence of God at times?

....

....

What must I hear so that I might trust that God is near?

....

....

....

....

....

....

DECEMBER 17

A family record of Jesus Christ, son of David. (Mt 1:1)

If we were to open an old family Bible, we might find a record of family births through several generations. It's rather significant that such records are kept in this copy of the Scriptures, the same book that holds the family record of Jesus Christ.

What has gone before us, in history, shapes the world of today. Who has gone before us, our personal history, does the same. It would be interesting to reach back to those earlier generations and touch the bits of influence they have had upon our lives. From whom did I inherit who I am today? To whom can I trace my roots, my unique inheritance?

As Christians, our uniqueness comes from Jesus Christ—Jesus, who reached into the history of the Scriptures and brought forth the essential characteristics of the spiritual life: love of God and love of neighbor. This is our inheritance as members of a Christian family tree. We are part of the birth of many generations who have drawn upon and flourished in the strength of these roots. Let us pray that we, too, will pass on this glorious and challenging legacy to those who follow us in Christ.

Prayer

Lord of generations,
all time has passed
before your sight.
You have given us,
year after year,
an inheritance
rich in mercy
and generous in love.

Be mindful
of your family
as we grow
through changing seasons
and passing years.
Let us not squander mercy
through self-righteous need,
nor love
through self-centered will.

May the waters
of our baptism
carry these gifts
and
flow with abundance—
pouring down
upon generations
yet to come....
Then will this grace
sustain in us
the memory
of our brother, Jesus Christ.
Amen.

Reflection

What are my gifts?

. . . .

. . . .

Who has influenced these in my life?

. . . .

. . . .

In what unique ways have I used them to influence the reign of God
in my world?

. . . .

. . . .

. . . .

DECEMBER 18

When Joseph awoke he did as the angel of the Lord directed him. (Mt 1:22)

Sometimes we feel quite burdened by the decisions we have to make. If we can slow ourselves down, we may come to the conclusion that we should give the problem a little more time—give it a rest for a little while . . . maybe even sleep on it. Joseph did. He probably gave his decision about Mary more time than we realize. He must have wrestled with his thoughts and feelings and realized there was no quick or easy solution.

As we walk this journey of life, we'd like things to be simple and clear. But they aren't. Yet, forcing our problems to a quick solution only pushes against a natural rhythm and flow. What we need is an "advent attitude" . . . the capacity to wait for the fullness. For it will come, but only when the time is right.

Emmanuel, God-with-us, came to birth at such a time. Or, more surely, it was the birth of Jesus that gave time its fullness—made it the perfect moment in history. Perhaps the decisions we must make will come in the same way, for the Spirit of God continues to birth human life. We can trust time—after all, God did.

Prayer

Lord of time,
teach us how
to trust the waiting.
Help us to
hope for fullness,
for we grow anxious
when concern is heavy
and only time will yield
the answer.

We know
some things need sleep,
but our rest
is often fitful.

We prefer to trust
ourselves,
and resist the uncontrollable.

Calm our fears
as we loosen our grasp
on time.
Give us faith
in divine wisdom,
openness
to gentle inspiration,
and courage
for this holy trust. Amen.

Reflection

What do I fear when I feel driven to find an answer or reach a conclusion quickly?

....
....
....
....
....

Can I trust the gift of time as coming from the wisdom of God? How might I help myself do that?

....
....
....
....
....

47

DECEMBER 19

Do not be frightened, your prayer has been heard. (Lk 1:13)

Zechariah was visibly shaken by the appearance of the angel Gabriel. As a messenger from God, Gabriel then proclaimed that the impossible was possible—Elizabeth would bear a son. Today we do not see angels, but perhaps the advent of a stranger with good news for our lives would make us equally skeptical.

Jesus came to this earth as a stranger. Few welcomed him, despite the fact that he brought the good news of God's love and life. Did they find this news so unbelievable.... Is that why they rejected him? Is the love of God and fullness of life so fantastic that, even today, we would reject these tidings of great joy? It is often difficult for us to accept the fact that we are accepted. We even argue with dear friends who know us so well. We even argue with God. What will it take to make us believers?

Prayer

God of gladness and joy,
you who first loved us,
forgive our unbelief
in the goodness
you created
within our hearts.

We have
such little faith
in ourselves.
We question
the faith you have
in us.
We want to believe,
but we fail
in our attempts
and fall short
of our ideals.

Forgive our painful strivings,
for we struggle
against
the freedom and joy
of your creation....
We struggle against
the freedom and joy
of our very selves.

Take our unbelief
and mold believing.
We accept
your gentle touch.
We accept acceptance,
and bow our heads
in humble gratitude.
Amen.

Reflection

Do I experience God's love for me? How?

....

....

....

....

Looking back on my life, who have borne this message of God's love?

....

....

....

Have I brought this message to others?

....

DECEMBER 20

In the sixth month, the angel Gabriel was sent from God to a town of Galilee named Nazareth. (Lk 1:26)

What is the word of God you are waiting for? The tension of longing heightens as we draw closer to the celebration of Christmas. Will we hear God's word to us then? Will it be dramatic or simple?

God's Word, Jesus Christ, is the underlying theme of all that we hope for and trust. Whatever our hearts long to hear is spoken in the Word-made-flesh. Human life is the language of God. And so, Jesus articulates divine love. It was divine love who sent Jesus to walk among us. That same Word of God leads us today. As the Word was sent forth from the mouth of God, so Jesus sends us forth.... "Come, follow me," he says. With Mary we pray, "Let it be done to me as you say."

Prayer

Word of Love,
issued forth
from the mouth
of God,
break open our deafness.
Enlighten our minds.
Strengthen our will.
Engage our hearts
that we might hear,
not only with
our ears,
but with the
fullness of our being.

We cry out to you
from depths
unfathomable
even to ourselves.

Our longing
is stretched paper-thin.
We need to know
the love and life-
language
you speak
to us each day.

Lead us to our loving God.
Bless us ...
embrace us
with arms of
courage and hope,
that we may walk
with you
along the path
of the ways of God. Amen.

Reflection

What word of God am I seeking today?
How might I prepare for that word?

....

....

What "good news" will I share with others?

....

....

Is there a word God seeks from me this day? What might it be?

....

....

....

DECEMBER 21

Blessed is she who trusted that the Lord's words to her would be fulfilled. (Lk 1:45)

Blessed are we who make space and place for the holy within.
Who kneel in prayer, and raise hearts and hands to God.
Blessed are we who admit in humility the truth of our poverty.
Who are open to possibilities and smile at the impossible.
Blessed are we who are present to the fullness of time.
Who extend hands of communion, healing threats of separation.
Blessed are we who have the strength to be weak.
Who live in waiting and surrender to the timeless.
Blessed are we who are free to allow visions and dreams to be.
Who welcome angels and trust in strangers.
Blessed are we who trust that the Lord's word to us will be fulfilled.

Prayer

Lord God,
give me the grace of today.
Free me from my
wanderings and wonderings.
Empty my cluttered mind,
releasing the confusion
of my private tower of Babel.
Loosen my grip on life
so that life may grasp me
and take me where it will.
Open my heart
when I bar its door,
preventing others from
  entering in.
Let me walk in the footsteps
of ordinary time
to enjoy the dance of each day.

Let there always be
a light in my eyes
to mirror your presence
in my soul ...
a smile on my lips
to welcome strangers
and laugh at the clowning
in this greatest show
  called earth,
a spirit of forgiveness
to heal the brokenness
I share with others ...
the grace of celebration
to remind me you are God ...
and a sense of peace, your peace,
to carry me through
the rhythm of today. Amen.

Reflection

Am I able to trust even when I feel the discomfort of powerlessness?

....

....

Do I see these difficult experiences as opportunities of grace?

....

....

....

Do I have preconceived notions as to how my trust in God will or must be fulfilled?

....

....

....

DECEMBER 22

Mary remained with Elizabeth about three months and then returned home. (Lk 1:56)

What thoughts went through Mary's mind while she stayed with her cousin Elizabeth? Surely she felt changes taking place. She must have noticed movement in the quiet sanctuary of her womb. Three months . . . but in many ways time stood still for Mary as she waited upon this mystery of new life.

Yet, this was only the beginning. Throughout her life Mary would wonder about her child, would live with mystery, again and again. The waiting would continue in the quiet of her heart, where she would ponder the meaning of this special life.

What calmed her fears and gave her courage while she waited? Mary believed that she was a part of something greater than herself . . . a larger plan . . . a vital part of the Mystery. Today, we call it salvation. Mary did not have a name for it, but that did not stop her from believing.

Prayer

Lord of mystery,
God of those who wait,
help us to live
in this womb of time
free of the need
to capture
what we do not
understand.

When darkness
envelops our lives,
and mystery stills
our knowing,
help us to make
peace
with what is yet
unnamed.

Teach us
wisdom of heart,
that we might
believe
without seeing,
trust
without knowing,
and live
with promise
in our hearts. Amen.

Reflection

When I find myself living with mystery, what thoughts go through my mind?

....

....

....

Am I able to see God at the center of this experience?

....

How can I become more comfortable with what is unnamed ... the mysteries I experience in my life? Can Mary be of help to me? How?

....

....

....

DECEMBER 23

When Elizabeth's time for delivery arrived, she gave birth to a son. Her neighbors and relatives... rejoiced. (Lk 1:57-58)

Today we celebrate the birth of a child. Isn't it true that a newborn baby catches everyone's eye? We can't wait to hold that child. We say things like: "How precious! How beautiful! How special!" Even today's reading reflects some of those feelings—"Neighbors and relatives rejoice." They exclaimed, "What will this child be? Was not the hand of the Lord upon him!" It is only natural to say and to do all these things because a newborn baby is a miracle of love . . . the creation of God . . . God's love made flesh!

If, every time we look at a newborn child, we think and feel these things, what happens when the child grows up? What happens when we grow up? Do we still look at ourselves, today, and say: precious, beautiful, special? Do we still think to ourselves: so filled with possibilities, goodness and love? Do we still acknowledge that the hand of the Lord is upon us? That we are God's love made flesh?

Once a year on that special day, our birth-day, do we still celebrate our creation—really celebrate it?

Prayer

God of Life,
before I was, you knew me.
You gazed on me with love
and rocked me in arms of hope.
Your wisdom saw beyond my present.
Your faith in me beheld the beauty.
You saw my greater truth,
and brought into being
creation, as you knew it.
What happened mattered not to you
as much as your belief in me.
Image and likeness would endure
the test of brokenness and time.
Believing does such things.
So today and every day,
I make my act of faith in you.
For long ago, with whispered breath,
you credoed me to life.

Reflection

What is precious, beautiful and special about me?

. . . .

. . . .

Do I appreciate the unique gift of God that I am?
Who helps me to do this?

. . . .

. . . .

. . . .

How can I help others to know they are a gift?

. . . .

. . . .

DECEMBER 24

Blessed be the Lord, the God of Israel, because he has visited his people and set them free. (Lk 1:68)

Jesus, our saving God, restored infinite possibilities to human life. And so we find, in our hearts, a deep desire to do the Father's will. But how can we be sure? Who I am, and how I respond to the tasks of my daily life, will lead me to the knowledge that I seek.

Have I valued the gift of life, seen my uniqueness and offered that to my brothers and sisters? Then I am doing God's will. Have I accepted the mystery of life, trusted its process and rhythm, seen myself as in the heart of God? Then I am doing God's will. Have I cried out in joy as well as in pain? Lifted my heart in praise and bowed before God in need? Then I am doing God's will. Have I opened my heart to love, my life to forgiveness, my spirit to compassion? Then I am doing God's will.

The holy mystery of God, ever present in life, is a saving mystery. We, too, will find peace if we continue to live this gospel of grace.

Prayer

Saving God,
Lord of possibilities,
enable us to reach
into the depths
of our spirits
and bring forth
the fullness of life.

Help us to be
who you created
us to be—
alive in Jesus Christ
your Son.
Let us embody him
who embodied you.

Let us not
run from life,
for it is there
that we find you.
May your saving grace
amaze us
in our everyday
dreams and realities.

May we hope in you
as you have
hoped in us.
And may we trust
in the goodness of life
that you have meant it to be.
Amen.

Reflection

How do I define God's will?

....

....

....

Does my definition bring me peace and hope or anxiety and concern?

....

What is it about the gift of life that I trust?

....

What is it that makes me fearful?

....

How could Jesus touch my fears and give me hope in life?

....

....

CHRISTMAS DAY   THE BIRTH

This day in David's city a Savior has been born to you, the Messiah and Lord. (Lk 2:11)

O Father of our Lord Jesus Christ—
is this any way for a king to be born?
I suppose you asked the same question
when the fullness of time came.
I don't think you wanted your Son
born in a stable, instead of a bed.
You took quite a chance with Joseph, too.
Did you know he'd come through
for you, for Mary and for us?
What faith you have!
You placed your Son in the arms
of a world who knew him not.
You gave your most precious gift
to us, who would be threatened
by so much goodness—
who would reject kindness and healing
and who would betray love itself.
But this didn't stop you
from loving, from hoping, from trusting.
So you let us
bungle through our mistakes—
even those made in the name of love,
even those made in your name . . .
the name of God.
You saw beyond the stable
and beyond the cross.
You saw believers as well as unbelievers.
You saw conversion in spite of sin.
You saw eternal life in the face of death.
You saw full circle in the emptiness of human hearts.

OF OUR LORD JESUS CHRIST

Is this any way for a king to be born?
Surely not,
but it really didn't matter, did it?
He was born
and continues to be born
in poverty.
He continues to live
with rejection and betrayal.
He continues to be nailed and crowned.
And,
he continues to burst through the tomb of death,
raise his face to the sun
and laugh resurrection—
a hearty laugh, a grateful laugh,
that breaks through the barriers
of time
and echoes in the souls
of those who believe.

Come, Lord Jesus!

FEAST OF THE HOLY FAMILY

Christ's peace must reign in your hearts. (Col 3:15)

Brother Jesus,
When the wound of betrayal cuts deeply into the human heart,
    may I anoint the tearing with your healing love.
When my brother or sister cannot travel beyond yesterday,
    may I lead them through the gates of fear.
When troubled waters wash over your little ones,
    may I be the anchor of faith in the depths of their souls.
When spirits struggle and lose their way,
    may I be a spark of inspiration that enlightens their minds.
When a dark cave seems the only dwelling place on this earth,
    may I be a candle on its innermost ledge.
When weeping overcomes our family in the loneliness of grief,
    may I soothe their anguished hearts with your embrace.
O Divine Master,
    grant that I may not so much
    seek comfort from others, as to comfort them;
    long for a kindred spirit, as to be a companion to all;
    cry out for love, as to cry out with love.
For it is in the gift of self that gifts are exchanged.
    It is in acceptance given that peace can be received.
    And it is in entering the darkness
    that we will become eternal light. Amen.

SOLEMNITY OF MARY, MOTHER OF GOD

Mary treasured all these things and reflected on them in her heart. (Lk 2:19)

O God, who drew me forth
    from nothingness,
My heart and soul sing out
    in celebration
    of your creative touch.

For your knowing of me
    brought a smile
    of blessing to your lips.
And in your gaze,
    what I thought poor
    is filled with richness
    beyond my dreams.

Only you could throw open
    the door of my heart
    and release your word
    within me.

And it is there
I hear—
Holy ... Holy ... Holy ...

Your compassion for me
    inspires mercy
    in my soul.
The truth of your presence
    brings me to my knees—
    for you shatter my illusions
    and remind me
    you are God.

Fantasies of self-perfection
    are emptied out,
    as you gift desire
    with an understanding heart.

You have not forsaken us
    when we have forgotten you.
Through generations
    we celebrate the eternal flame
    of your love.
For your promise to Abraham
    and Sarah
    continues to birth new life
    in us who believe.

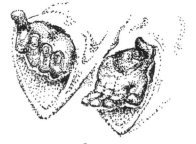

EPIPHANY *The Manifestation of the Lord*

Rise up in splendor, Jerusalem! Your light has come. . . .
(Is 60:1)

Holy Light,
searcher of the human heart,
guide and beacon
of eternal hope—
pour your radiance
into our very souls.
Brighten the darkness
within. . . .
Enlighten our minds.
Open our hearts.
Lift our spirits
that we may touch
the rays of your
divine love
flowing through
and around us.

We offer
the simple cup
of human life
as gold—
fired and fashioned
by the love
of Jesus, the Christ.

We lift
our hearts,
the incense of prayer—
to praise
your divine wisdom
revealed
in shepherd simplicity.

We bring
our desire for you
as myrrh—
preserving, enriching,
sustaining
the hope of new life.

Lead us
to that light
within,
that we may
be light
to one another . . .
and make manifest
your saving love.
Amen.

BAPTISM OF OUR LORD

"I should be baptized by you," John protested. "Yet you come to me!" (Mt 3:14)

And so it is, Lord . . .
Mystery.
Let me rest in this thing
called "mystery."
Let me see it less as a threat
and more as an invitation.
An invitation to adventure
and freedom.
An invitation to love.

Because you are the mystery, Lord.
You are its heart and soul.
So, to stand at its threshold,
to look into the depths of its eyes,
is to be present to you.

Why fear falling, then?
For to stumble in the darkness
has the possibility
of being caught in your embrace.

Give me the grace
to fly with the mystery . . .
to dance to its rhythm . . .
or, at times, to sit . . .
just sit in its presence.
For in you,
darkness and light are the same. Amen.

And God replies:

> I believe in you—
> the reflection of my glory,
> co-creator of the kingdom,
> and child of my love, my blessed one.
> —conceived by grace,
> my word made flesh . . .
> who suffers because of the poverty
> within your human beauty,
> and the frailty of a world
> that stands on tiptoe anticipation . . .
> groaning and longing
> for the birth of new life.
>
> I believe in you—
> who are called to share
> the death and darkness
> of the grain of wheat,
> who at times
> experience the depths
> only to know the height,
> breath and life of resurrection—

at home with me,
sharing the joy of the son
who heals and brings peace
in his loving embrace.

You live
in the presence
of my breath of life,
whose hushed whispers
you have welcomed
into the corners of your heart.
You dwell with sisters and brothers
beyond the boundaries of your home.
Many have prayed for you,
far beyond your imagination ...
enabling you to know forgiveness
and offer mercy.

Now, go and live
because ...
I believe in you!